Festivals

CARNIVAL

Jon Mayled

Wayland

Festivals

Carnival
Christmas
Commemorative Festivals
Easter
Hallowe'en
Harvest and Thanksgiving
New Year
Buddhist Festivals
Hindu Festivals
Jewish Festivals
Muslim Festivals
Sikh Festivals

Editor: Penny McDowell

First published in 1987 by
Wayland (Publishers) Limited
61 Western Road, Hove
East Sussex BN3 1JD, England

© Copyright 1987 Wayland (Publishers) Limited

British Library Cataloguing in Publication Data

Mayled, Jon
  Carnival. – (Festivals).
  1. Carnival. – Juvenile literature
  I. Title   II. Series
  394.2′5   GT4180

  ISBN 1–85210–019–2

Phototypeset by Kalligraphics Ltd, Redhill, Surrey
Printed in Italy by G. Canale & C.S.p.A, Turin
Bound in the U.K. at The Bath Press, Avon

Contents

Carnival

Carnivals are happy occasions. They are times when people stop work and go out into the streets to sing, dance and enjoy themselves. Different types of carnival, celebrating different events, take place all over the world.

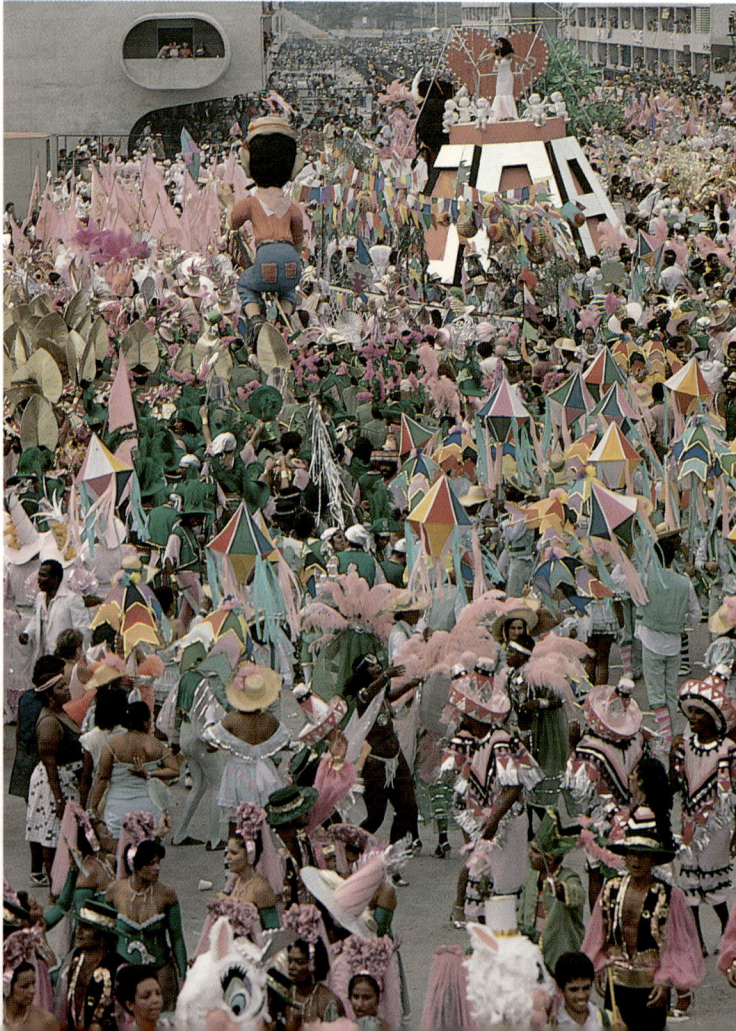

Carnival in Rio de Janeiro is the main event of the year in the life of many of the people of that city.

The word carnival itself comes from the Latin words *carnem levare* – meaning to take away meat and so *carnelevarium*. Later this was changed to *carnevale*, by the Italians, meaning 'farewell to meat'.

Carnevale was a preparation for the Christian season of Lent, the forty days before Easter, when people did not eat meat. The main events of carnival have always taken place on Shrove Tuesday which is often called Mardi Gras meaning Fat Tuesday.

Lent begins on Ash Wednesday which can fall on any date between 7 February and 9 March. In the past carnival would begin as early as the Feast of the Epiphany on 6 January, but today it usually lasts no more than two to three days.

Carnival was originally a final feast before the forty-day fast of Lent. It is still celebrated in many different ways, especially in Catholic countries, all over the world.

Pancake races are a traditional part of many Shrove Tuesday celebrations in Britain.

5

However, the origins of these events are probably much older than Christianity itself. In order to persuade people to convert to Christianity, the Church took over the practices of some of the earlier pagan festivals and attached them to Christian feast days. One of these was the Roman festival of Saturnalia.

This was a mid-winter celebration when Romans honoured Saturn, the god of seedtime and harvest. Saturnalia was a public holiday which lasted for a whole week. There were feasts and games and for a day slaves were free to do as they wished. Each year a man was chosen to represent Saturn and was treated like a god. However, at the end of the festival he was put to death.

This treatment of slaves as equals is similar to the medieval Feast of Fools. Once a year, usually around Christmas time, people made up sharp, critical songs about those in authority and ridiculed the most solemn and respected traditions and individuals. This custom has found its

This seventeenth century engraving shows an egg dance in Holland. This was a Dutch custom, performed at Easter time.

Since the 1950s steel bands, such as this one in Tobago, have provided the music for calypso singers during carnival.

way into calypso music where the words are as important as the music and rhythm. Another tradition connected with the Feast of Fools involved the choosing of a boy on 6 December who would be a mock 'bishop' for three weeks.

Many ancient traditions have formed what we now think of as carnival. All over Europe in the Middle Ages there were examples of the Battle of Summer and Winter. Actors played the parts of Summer and Winter, and a contest was held in which Summer conquered Winter. This was to ensure the coming of spring and the new year's growth and harvest. At the end of the event, sheaves of corn were buried – this was called 'burying the carnival'.

From this we can see that carnival, as it is now celebrated, is a mixture of many wintertime events. Although the Church permitted carnival as a final celebration before the beginning of the Lent fast, it incorporates many older ideas of new life and fertility. Some of these ancient traditions can still be seen in carnival today.

The Battle of Flowers

In Italy, carnival is celebrated in many different ways. The towns of Viareggio (on the north-west coast) and San Remo (near the French-Italian border) have large carnival floats. Carnival in Venice has been revived in recent years. The magnificent procession of Venetians wearing stunning costumes and masks, parading to St. Mark's Square, is not only a colourful and stunning sight, but a time when both rich and poor people can be equal.

These masked figures are taking part in the carnival celebrations in Venice.

On the Sunday before the first day of Lent there is the procession of *Boeuf Gras* (fat beef), when animals are led through the streets by costumed butchers. On Shrove Tuesday people, in costume, walk through the streets carrying lighted tapers. They do their best to keep their own alight while trying to blow out other people's.

This figure of a bull is part of the Boeuf Gras *procession at Mèze Hérault in France.*

In the processions in Rome and Venice people throw flowers at each other. The throwing of foliage or flowers is part of many ancient fertility rites and carries the same idea of good luck as the throwing of rice or confetti at a wedding.

This Battle of Flowers was taken up in the Tournament of Roses held in Pasadena, California, USA, from 1890. Also, on Jersey in the Channel Islands, there is an annual Battle of Flowers held on the second Thursday in August. Huge carts tour the streets decorated with models

The Venice carnival is famous for its beautiful and extravagant costumes and masks.

made of flowers. At the end of the procession people rip the carts apart and throw the flowers at each other.

There is also a tradition of throwing flowers in Nice, France, where a statue of King Carnival appears at the *mi-carême*, mid-Lent festival.

The Battle of Flowers is a lively and popular August event on the Channel Island of Jersey.

Devils and Drums

In parts of Spain, such as Valencia and San Fermín in Pamplona, huge papier-mâché figures known as *Gigantes y Cabezudos* (giants with bigheads) appear in the carnival processions. They represent important historical characters. Some

Figures with huge heads, like these in Madrid, feature strongly at carnival celebrations in Spain.

These children in traditional dress are taking part in the carnival procession in Wels, Austria.

processions have figures of King Ferdinand and Queen Isabella of Spain, who united their country against the Moorish invaders and finally drove them out in 1492. Other figures dress as Moors and sometimes a mock battle is staged between the two groups. The figures originally represented the much older traditional theme of the Battle of Summer and Winter.

Diablos y muertos (devils and deaths) are shown as comic figures. This is the same tradition as the morality plays of the Middle Ages in England when Bible stories were acted out in the streets.

There are also figures dressed as shepherdesses, wearing white dresses. These are accompanied by people with animal masks who are said to be from the Garden of Eden.

Figures dressed as ghosts, witches and death also appear in carnival processions in Innsbruck and Imst in Austria. They parade through the streets to the music of drums, whips and bull-roarers.

Giants and Kisses

Carnival is celebrated all over Germany and Austria. Even small towns have their *Fasching* or carnival celebrations.

In both Germany and Switzerland groups of masked actors go from house to house performing plays during carnival, rather like carol singers at Christmas time.

Masks such as these being worn at Rottweil in West Germany are an important feature of carnival all over the world.

In the Rhineland it is called *Karneval*. The celebrations begin at the eleventh hour of the eleventh day of the eleventh month, which is St. Martin's Day, and continue until Ash Wednesday – *Aschermittwoch*. There is dancing, street parades, parties and costume balls and at this time of the year you may kiss anyone.

In Bavaria, months of planning go into the events and competitions which are held at this time. The main *Fasching* celebrations are in the city of Munich, West Germany, where once again huge carnival giants are carried through the streets. These giants also appear in Cologne where beer festivals form part of the celebrations.

These children, with their paper lanterns, are celebrating St. Martin's Day, the beginning of Karneval *in the Rhineland.*

There are few traditional Shrove Tuesday celebrations left in England apart from pancake races. People race through the streets tossing pancakes as they run. Pancakes were originally made as a way of using up eggs, milk and flour, foods which could not be eaten during the fast of Lent.

The celebrations for carnival are often based on very old traditions. This picture is of a folklore procession at Kehl in Bavaria.

However, there is a tradition of playing a type of football in the streets at this time which still continues in some villages in the countryside. There appear to be no rules to these games with their huge teams and often people can be injured. This seems to be part of a much older custom which is similar to some of the carnival practices from other countries.

These girls are celebrating the flower festival in Portugal. Flowers have become an important part of carnival in many countries.

Carnival! – Playing Mask

New Orleans

The Mardi Gras, 'Fat Tuesday', celebrations in France reached the American city of New Orleans in 1827 when French students settled there. The first decorated floats appeared in 1837 and carnival parades became an annual event in 1857.

Magnificent decorated floats in the Mardi Gras celebrations in New Orleans, Louisiana, USA.

In the early nineteenth century, black slaves in New Orleans were free on Sundays to sing and dance together in a field called Congo Square. However, after the slave rebellions of the mid-1800s, blacks were forbidden to assemble except during Mardi Gras.

The native South Americans, who are sometimes called Indians, sheltered runaway slaves. Because of this, many of the black groups in the New Orleans Mardi Gras appear as Indians and are called such names as the *Wild Tchoupitoulas*.

Jazz is the traditional music of carnival in New Orleans.

Carnival is a very important event in New Orleans which has been called 'the city that care forgot'.

Men and women sew the costumes. Each year after Mardi Gras the costumes are disassembled and new ones are made at great personal expense as each group tries to outdo the others in beauty and originality.

The music of carnival in New Orleans is jazz and there are band floats and street dancing. As well as the 'Indians' there are the traditional figures of devils, people wearing fantastic masks, many wonderful costumes and pageant figures.

As the floats pass by, people sometimes throw tokens to the watching crowds. These are usually strings of cheap, brightly coloured beads or plastic coins bearing the name of the group of people responsible for the float.

Street music and dancing are a very important aspect of carnival in New Orleans.

Rio de Janeiro

Carnival in Rio has been described as the eighth wonder of the world.

Here, the African roots of the people are still very strong. Many came as slaves from Angola in south-west Africa, and some of the people still worship African gods. These are honoured in the same way as African monarchs of the past. Slaves from western Nigeria have brought their own religion and gods with them and spiritual tribal

There are many samba schools in Rio de Janeiro. This picture is of the Beija Flor School at the Rio carnival.

medicine is still practised. In the church of St. Francis, people who have been cured leave 'ex-voto' offerings for healing. These are models of the infected limbs.

Carnival is very important to the people of Brazil. The majority of its people suffer terrible poverty, but at carnival time, they are able to forget everything and take to the streets to dance, sing and enjoy themselves.

This shanty town in Brazil is typical of the homes of many of its people.

Carnival lasts for the three days before the beginning of Lent. There are sixteen 'schools' (groups usually from the same neighbourhood) who take part in the carnival. The oldest of them still in existence is the Manqueira school which was started in 1928 and has 4,000 members divided into fifty sections. The school spends £500,000 a year on carnival. Some of this money comes from the city while the rest is raised by promoters. The fantastic floats and costumes, which cost at least £30 each, are made by professional craftsmen.

In 1985, this carnival cup was won by the Mocidade samba school. Every year a prize is given to the best school.

The music of carnival in Rio is the Samba. The dance of the same name is performed to this music and is made up of tilting and rocking motions of the body. In the parade the samba is usually danced in groups, but can be danced in couples. Today, the parade is as much for the tourists as for the local people. Brazil is the largest Catholic country in the world and after twenty-one years of military rule the people of Rio are poor. They see this as God's will, but everyone is equal at carnival and judged only on their ability to parade. Points are given under ten

Above *The city of Rio de Janeiro is world famous for its carnival celebrations.*

Below *The samba dancers spend a great deal of money on their fabulous carnival costumes.*

headings including songs, choreography, floats and rhythm.

Carnival is also celebrated in the Brazilian cities of Salvador, Recife and São Paulo.

Preparations and rehearsals for carnival in Rio de Janeiro begin as soon as the previous year's event is over.

These voodoo worshippers, with their colourful costumes, are taking part in the carnival celebrations of Haiti in the West Indies.

Haiti

When European plantation owners went to the West Indies they took carnival there with them.

A major religion of the island of Haiti is Voodoo although eight out of ten people there belong to the Catholic church.

Carnival in Haiti owes a great deal to the African heritage of its people. The carnival figures represent African gods, the 401 Voodoo spirits which control the universe and important Haitian figures such as Toussaint L'Ouverture. He is the national hero who in 1804 established the world's first black republic.

Martinique

On the French island of Martinique, carnival or *Vaval* begins on Ash Wednesday morning. It ends when the coffin of King Vaval (an adaptation of the word carnival), is buried. This custom appears to date back to the 'burying the carnival' ceremonies which were held hundreds of years ago in Europe.

This children's carnival in Aruba is an important part of the celebrations in the Dutch Antilles.

Trinidad and Tobago

The most famous West Indian carnival is the one which is held every year on the island of Trinidad.

The Spanish arrived in Trinidad in 1498 and the island was finally captured from them by the British in 1797. For many years it had been a Catholic country and the tradition of carnival was well established. At first, carnival was just for the white people of the islands and always ended with a fancy dress ball. Many of the Europeans dressed as slaves. Freed men were allowed to wear masks in the street but the slaves were not.

The merry-making was a fairly quiet and orderly affair but in 1833 slavery was ended and the festival became a celebration for the newly-freed people. Carnival was very important to these people. It was an opportunity for them to express their freedom in music, particularly the beating of drums which had been previously forbidden, and to be critical of their society in their songs. They could also express their identity and culture at this time. At first they copied the fine dress of their former masters and mistresses and some wore white flesh-coloured masks. Later, however, the processions began to include figures from other countries. Pirates, Turks, native South Americans – Amerindians – and Scottish highlanders appeared among the costumes.

There are also other traditional characters who can still be seen in the processions today. These include *Moco Jumbie*, a West African figure on stilts, *Jab Jab* or *Jab Molassi*, a devil with a long whip who is covered with molasses, and *Burroquite*, a figure whose costume suggests that he is riding a horse.

The time for the start of carnival in Trinidad was fixed in 1849 so that the processions could not begin before midnight on Sunday. This was the beginning of *Lundi Gras* (Fat Monday) which merged with the old August festival of *Canbouley*. This name comes from the French *cannes brulées* meaning burnt canes. Whenever there was a fire in the sugar plantations the slaves from the area were sent to put it out. They took long sticks or canes with them. *Canbouley* became a procession of torches, drumming, dancing and stick fights or *calenda*. This ritual became very important to slaves, as it was the only excitement in their dull lives.

Carnival is the main event of the year in Port of Spain, Trinidad.

The riots of 1881 resulted in the banning of slaves carrying sticks, and the carnival could now not begin before 6am on Monday morning. In 1883, drumming was banned and, because the processions had become so violent, in 1884 carnival itself was banned for a long time.

The music of the Trinidad carnival is *Kaiso* or calypso. The name is thought possibly to have come from the West African word *Kaiso* which means 'well done'.

The first singer of *Kaiso* was Gros Jean, the African slave of a French master St. Hilaire Bugarant – who was the chief magistrate. In the south of France there was still the tradition of rich people employing a fool or jester. It was in this way that Gros Jean was taught to sing songs which brought his master's neighbours into disrepute.

Months of rehearsals and costume making are involved to create the impressive carnival processions in Trinidad.

Calypso is vital to Trinidad carnival and, more recently, to other countries. From January onwards more than a hundred singers will meet in the halls called tents where they compete for the title of Calypso King or Queen. People judge the songs on their music and the words which are traditionally topical, satirical songs about modern life. The singers choose names for themselves. Two of the most famous recent kings are Lord Kitchener and the Mighty Sparrow. Every year one calypso is chosen as the carnival song.

Winston Spree Simon invented the first steel drums in Trinidad in 1945. Since then hundreds of steel bands have formed, like this one in the Bahamas.

Although these songs are often very critical of the government and its ministers, people enjoy them and it is said that, 'The Prime Minister will never take a calypso man to court.'

Because the drumming was once banned, people had to find other ways of making music. At first they used bamboo stems which were cut to different lengths and widths. The *foulé* was the smallest, the medium length one was called the *cutter* which was beaten with a stick, and the longest one, the *boom*, is beaten on the ground. With these instruments people formed Tamboo Bamboo Bands. Even these were banned from time to time because it was feared the sticks might be used as weapons.

These costumed dancers in the French West Indies, are enjoying the music and activity of carnival.

People also used African drums, a stringed instrument called a *banjee*, a *chac-chac*, the salt-box bass, the Dutch gin flask and spoon and the tin kettle drum.

Carnival was banned during the Second World War but at the victory celebrations, on 6 May 1945, a new sound was heard – the steel band. These bands had been developed by Winston Spree Simon in one of the poorest areas of the island's capital, Port of Spain, and were made from steel oil drums. The top of the drum is beaten and tuned by a process of heating and hammering. They come in four main sizes: ping pongs which are the melody pans and are so-called because they can produce thirty-two different notes, guitar and cello pans for the harmony and tune booms for the bass. At first the drums were carried around the players' necks in processions. Later they were played on stands on large carnival floats.

Carnival is an opportunity for everyone, rich or poor, to dance, sing and enjoy themselves.

Today there are more than a hundred steel bands in the carnival, each having up to eighty or more members. The members are not only musicians. There is a king and queen and many masqueraders, and each band's dress is influenced by a particular theme.

In Trinidad and Tobago the carnival lasts for two days. In Port of Spain, on the Sunday before Lent, *Dimanche Gras* (Fat Sunday) the king and queen of carnival are crowned.

Carnival starts at 4am on Monday morning, the day before Shrove Tuesday. The beginning of carnival is called *Jouvay*. This comes from a French phrase *Le jour est ouvert* – 'the day is open', or 'it's a free for all'.

Musicians like these in Jamaica are a vital part of carnival celebrations all over the world.

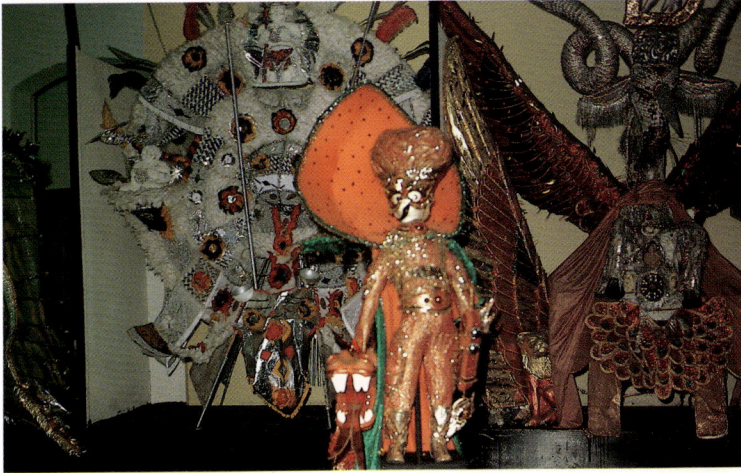

These fantastic carnival costumes are on display in a museum in Port of Spain, Trinidad.

For the next two days people spend their time in the streets dancing to the music of the bands 'playing mask'. Mask comes from the French word masquerade meaning a fancy dress ball.

On the first day, many traditional carnival figures appear in the streets. Witches, ghosts and devils are followed by people in traditional costumes and pageant figures from history.

Tuesday, Mardi Gras itself, is the day when the fabulous costumes of carnival appear. Every year people spend months designing and making their costumes in their workshops or mask camps. The costume bands may have thousands of members, masqueraders and musicians.

As many as a hundred thousand people parade in costumes and the groups are led by steel bands. People jump with the bands in the streets, sing, eat, drink and listen to calypsos in the tents.

Prizes are given for the best costumes and bands, and the singing and dancing continues far into the night which is lit up by fireworks. Carnival ends with the 'last lap' at midnight on Tuesday and then, Lent begins.

The Notting Hill Carnival

From the 1950s onwards many people from the West Indies came to live in England, and especially in London. They brought with them the tradition of carnival. Every year since 1961, on the Summer Bank Holiday which falls on the last weekend in August, costumed masqueraders and floats together with steel bands take over the streets of London's Notting Hill area. The weather is usually warm and this is perhaps the first time that the traditional carnival has been celebrated away from Lent.

Since 1961, the Notting Hill carnival has been an important and colourful event for the West Indian community in London.

The late Bob Marley, who was responsible for the recognition and popularity of reggae music.

Many of London's West Indian population have their roots in Jamaica. In the 1940s and 1950s the old Jamaican 'mento' music was influenced by Black American music and produced a rhythm called 'ska'. In turn this was slowed down to 'rock steady', from which came 'reggae' which, with its great performers such as Bob Marley, has become the predominant sound of the Notting Hill Carnival. All the ingredients of carnival are there – the food, masks, souvenirs and the all-pervading sound of the steel bands.

Another West Indian carnival is Caribana which started in Toronto, in Canada, in 1967. Like Notting Hill, it takes place in the warmer weather of August. The majority of Canada's West Indian population comes from Trinidad and so it is the calypso music which dominates the festivities of Caribana.

Juggernauts and Dragons

There are many other events similar to carnival which take place all over the world.

In June or July, the great *Ratha-Jatra* or *Jagannath* festival is held in the city of Puri in Orissa, India. This is a festival honouring the Hindu god *Krishna* who is called *Jagannath*.

On the second day of the month of *Ashadha* the statues of *Jagannath*, his sister *Subhadra* and brother *Balarama* are brought out of the temple newly-painted. They are placed on huge wooden carts which are up to 15 m high. Hundreds of

These children are wearing specially made costumes for the carnival in Toronto, Canada.

Huge floats are part of this parade in Adelaide, Australia.

people pull the carts through the streets to another temple. Then, after a few days, people pull them back to their original home. The English word juggernaut comes from this festival.

Yuan Tan, the Chinese New Year, is one of the brightest religious festivals in those countries where there is a Chinese community.

The festival takes place in January or February on the first day of the first lunar month. A week before, everyone gathers together to worship the kitchen god of their home, Tsao Wang, as on this night he is said to go to the Jade Emperor in heaven and report on each person's behaviour. Some people smear the lips of his picture with honey so that he can only say sweet things about them. The picture is then burnt to ensure that he gets to heaven – the rising smoke is said to help his ascent. One week later, on Chinese New Year's Eve, he returns and a new picture of him is put up. He is welcomed back into the home with firecrackers.

The shops close for three days on Chinese New Year's Eve and everyone tries to ensure that all their debts are paid before the New Year begins. Children are given new clothes and gifts of 'lucky money'.

Banners and dragons are a traditional part of the celebrations for Chinese New Year, shown here in the Soho area of London.

The New Year celebrations last for fifteen days and many of these have a carnival atmosphere. On the first and second days many firecrackers are let off. In some parts of China there is a parade of banners on the third day. On the thirteenth and fourteenth nights people carry beautifully carved and decorated lanterns through the streets.

However, it is the events of the fifteenth day which people especially associate with the Chinese New Year. Huge Chinese dragons take to the streets. These fabulous animals are made from bamboo, covered with brightly coloured cloth and paper. Some of them are up to 30 m long and need many people under them to perform their traditional dances. With the dragon are the Chinese lions who are his guardians. The dragon in Chinese mythology represents long life, prosperity and rain, and the lion represents good fortune. The streets are full of people dancing, listening to the music and watching the performance.

This dragon dance is taking place at the Chinese New Year festivities in Singapore.

41

There are many street carnivals held in Britain such as the carnivals at Lewes, Leeds and Bridgwater. There are also many local festivals which celebrate historical events of the area.

The processions include bands, walking costumed groups and huge floats. Like the carnivals in other parts of the world, an enormous amount of effort and time is taken to perfect the costumes and floats.

Firework displays are often to be found at British carnivals. The end of the carnival is sometimes declared with a spectacular show of catherine wheels, bangers, rockets, roman candles, sparklers and firecrackers. Fireworks are also popular all over the world at festivals and carnival celebrations.

Opposite *Large firework displays are often the final celebrations to mark the end of carnival.*

Below *The carnival in Leeds is one of the many street processions held in Britain.*

Glossary

Banjee A simple stringed instrument similar to a banjo.

Bull-roarer A thin, flat, pointed piece of wood attached to a 60 cm long cord, which is swung above the head to produce a whirring sound.

Chac-chac An instrument made from small dried gourds – a large, fleshy fruit with a hard rind – which are hollowed-out and filled with dried seeds.

Epiphany A Christian feast day on 6 January (Twelfth Night) which celebrates the Three Wise Men bringing gifts to the infant Jesus in the stable in Bethlehem.

Folklore The customs and traditions of the people of a region or country.

Lent The forty days before the Christian festival of Easter, which begins on Ash Wednesday. Traditionally Christians did not eat meat during this period and all rich foods were finished on Shrove Tuesday.

Magistrate A person who has the power to enforce laws.

Moors Muslims who invaded and ruled part of Spain from the eighth century AD. They were finally driven out in 1492 by King Ferdinand and Queen Isabella.

Morality plays Medieval street theatre. Religious stories were acted out on carts in the towns. The purpose was to provide education about Christianity for the spectators through an often comic presentation of the stories.

Pagan A member of any religious group other than Christianity or a person of no religion.

Satirical Words or lyrics to a play or song which make fun of important people in the church or society.

Shanty town A town, or an area of a town, where the people are very poor and live in extremely basic homes called shanties.

Tableau A group of people, in costumes, who stand completely still to illustrate a scene from history.

Tapers Thin wooden or waxen strips used like torches and to transfer flames.

Voodoo An ancient religious belief with many spirits or gods. An African religious cult involving witchcraft, mainly practised in the West Indies.

Further reading

Bancroft, *Chinese New Year* (RMEP, 1984)

Bennett, Olivia, *Carnival* (Macmillan Educational, 1986)

Blackwood, Alan, *New Year* (Wayland, 1985)

Davidson, *Shrove Tuesday, Ash Wednesday and Mardi Gras* (RMEP, 1984)

Frazer, Sir J. G., *The Golden Bough* (Macmillan, 1936)

Harris, Wilson, *Carnival* (Faber, 1985)

Harrowven, Jean, *Origins of Festivals and Feasts* (Kaye & Ward, 1980)

Menter, Ian, *Carnival* (Hamish Hamilton, 1982)

Morris, N. & Morris, T., *Carnival Time* (Hodder, 1985)

Picture Acknowledgements

The publisher would like to thank all those who provided pictures on the following pages: Bruce Coleman cover, 27; Cephas 42; J. Allan Cash Ltd 11, 31, 34, 35, 36, 43, 44, 45; Tony Morrison/South American Pictures 4, 21, 22, 23, 24 (bottom); Topham 7, 9, 10, 12, 13, 16, 32, 33, 37; Wayland 6; MacQuitty International 42; ZEFA 5, 8, 14, 15, 17, 18, 19, 20, 24 (top), 25, 26, 29, 30, 39, 40.

Index